WOMAN EVOLVE

BREAK UP WITH
YOUR FEARS
&
REVOLUTIONIZE
YOUR LIFE

STUDY GUIDE + SIX SESSIONS

SARAH JAKES ROBERTS

HarperChristian Resources

Woman Evolve Study Guide

© 2022 by Sarah Jakes Roberts

Requests for information should be addressed to:

HarperChristian Resources, 3900 Sparks Dr. SE, Grand Rapids, Michigan 49546

ISBN 978-0-310-15482-2 (softcover)

ISBN 978-0-310-15483-9 (ebook)

HarperChristian Resources titles may be purchased in bulk for church, business, fundraising, or ministry use. For information, please e-mail ResourceSpecialist@ChurchSource.com.

First Printing October 2022 / Printed in the United States of America

CONTENTS

WOMAN EVOLVE

My daughter, Makenzie, invited her friend, Sunday, to our home. The weather was finally pleasant after a few weeks of cold and rain. The moment Sunday's toe crossed the threshold of the kitchen my daughter Makenzie came barreling toward me. She'd just gotten her hair done, but I knew the moment she looked me in my eyes that she was going to ask one question: "Can I get my hair wet?"

Now, this may not seem like a big deal for some of you, but every Black woman knows that the Jeopardy music should have cued the moment the question was tossed in my direction. The hours of detangling, washing, conditioning, blow-drying, and pressing would go out of the window in a splash—literally! This is exactly why most Black women avoid wetting their freshly done hair.

Everything in me knew better. I thought about the time that would go into detangling, washing, conditioning, and styling her hair again. I also knew that as a homeschooled, middle child she often lacks fulfilling connection with girls her age. With a shoulder shrug, deep visceral sigh, an eye roll, and neck rub I told her the decision was hers to make.

I knew there were only two possible outcomes: Makenzie's hair remains intact, or I roll up my sleeves and restore whatever is damaged. With absolutely zero hesitation, my daughter stripped off her clothing, revealing a bathing suit she had on all along. One day we'll have to talk about the level of faith that her hidden bathing suit required! She took off full speed toward the swimming pool.

Right as Sunday cannonballed into the pool, Kenzie came running back in my direction with a look of pure horror in her eyes. "Mom, Sunday has never seen my natural hair!" Quick hair lesson for those who may not know: My daughter's mid-length straightened tresses would recoil into a teeny-weeny afro the moment her hair was submerged in water. A phenomenon known as shrinkage that evidently affected more than her hair. What she said was a concern about her hair, but what I heard was the fear of being fully seen.

Right in front of my eyes I witnessed my daughter's joy, confidence, hope, and faith shrivel. She was afraid that the love and adoration cultivated through their friendship would not withstand raw authenticity. Even more concerning was that my daughter wasn't convinced that she is as beautiful in her raw state as she is when her hair is altered to look a certain way.

If we dared to be honest, we'd confess that the fear of being seen is not just a little girl's struggle. It grows with us like a companion in every stage of life. Have you ever chosen to actively resist experiences, memories, or situations because you did not want to run the risk of being seen in your most vulnerable state? What if everyone around you knew about the depression? The addiction? Chronic stress? That troubled child? Heartbreak? What if you were truly seen?

When Adam and Eve were in the garden, they were so determined to not be seen in the aftermath of their sin that they used fig leaves and hid from each other, even though they both knew what the other had done (Genesis 3:7).

This is how so many of us go through life. Even our most intimate relationships are not granted access to our deep worry, shame, and concern. Don't get me wrong, I understand how deeply troubling it can be to share the thoughts and memories you can barely express to yourself, let alone to another. However, if we're truly going to experience the goodness of God, we must learn to remove the fig leaves we've come to love and exchange them for the covering that God wants to give us.

A woman who is determined to abandon what was must commit to the vulnerable process of evolving. It's impossible to maximize the potential that God has placed in each of us and stay the same. When we make room for transformation in our lives, we embody the definition of evolving.

Evolve means to develop gradually, especially from a simple to a more complex form. Notice how in saying *evolve* very slowly, you hear *Eve*. That's how much her experience has inspired me.

Eve made a mistake, but she had proper perspective on how important it was to course correct. She didn't settle for seeing life through a filter of fear, shame, or disappointment. *No!* She showed up and fought back. Her mistake never changed God's intention, only how He would fulfill that intention. God still desired to partner with Eve to unleash His divinity on earth—just as He wants to partner with you and me to bring heaven to earth today!

Whether you're attempting to recover from a setback, break free from an addiction, or bring forth good fruit despite the forbidden fruit you were exposed to, God has a redeeming plan for you—just like He did Eve. He's got plans and purposes that are beyond what you can imagine. He wants to bless you and bless people through you. You, yes you, are a beautiful, vast, ornate demonstration of God's thoughts and hope for humanity. And God is inviting you to take a risk and jump in the pool of grace. Let the living water change you from the inside out.

I'll never forget the joy my daughter had on her face that day when she jumped into the pool. You know what else? I'll never forget the joy she had on display as the world around her received an invitation to experience her most authentic self.

My hope and prayer is that through this study, you'll see you were born to bring light to the darkness, a revolution of faith to future generations, and a smile in the wild. And when the fear tries to creep in and the anxiety fights to find a way through, you'll remember two words, and read them as a command: *Woman, Evolve!*

Now, let's go change the world!

xo Sarah Jakes
Roberts

HOW TO USE THIS GUIDE

The *Woman Evolve* study guide is divided into six sessions. Every session includes Opening Discussion, Video Teaching Notes, Group Discussion Questions, a Closing Prayer, and Between Sessions Personal Study. As a group, you should plan to discuss the opening questions, watch the video, and then use the video notes and questions to engage with the topic of each session. There is complete freedom to decide how to best use these elements to meet the needs of your group. The goal of doing any small group study is to develop relationships with one another and a deeper personal relationship with God—consider the material in the videos and this study guide to be the catalyst for both!

GROUP SIZE

This six-session small group video study is designed to be experienced in a group setting such as a Bible study, Sunday school class, retreat, or online gathering. If your gathering is large, you may want to consider splitting everyone into smaller groups of five to eight people. This will ensure that everyone has enough time to participate in discussions while encouraging healthy engagement and growth.

If you are solo, a party of one, consider yourself part of the greater Woman Evolve movement of women across the country. Consider using the group discussion questions as inspiration for conversation with friends, family members, colleagues, or other women you have relationships with on a regular basis in your life. This content is meant for all women, and you might find simply asking a friend a few of these questions will lead to deeper and greater friendship as well as an opportunity to share this study with another.

MATERIALS NEEDED

Everyone will need a copy of this study guide, which includes personal streaming access to all the teaching videos. Instructions for accessing the videos and the personal access code are located on the inside front cover of each study guide. Don't forget to write down your password! You will simply log in each time you want to watch a video or catch up if you miss a group meeting.

Each session of this study guide includes opening questions to discuss, notes for the video teachings, directions for activities and discussion questions, and personal Bible studies to work through in between group meetings.

Having your own copy of the book *Woman Evolve* will take your experience of this study to a new level. The videos and content in this study guide are based on the book.

TIMING

The timing notations—for example, 20 minutes—indicate the actual length of the video segments and the suggested times for each activity or discussion. Within your allotted time, you may not get to all the discussion questions. Remember that the *quantity* of questions addressed isn't as important as the *quality* of the discussion.

FACILITATION

Your group will need to choose a person to serve as a facilitator. This person will be responsible for starting the video and keeping track of time during discussions and activities. Facilitators may also read questions aloud and monitor discussions, prompting everyone in the group to respond, and assuring that everyone has the opportunity to participate.

PERSONAL STUDY IN BETWEEN GROUP MEETINGS

During the week, you can maximize the impact of this content with the personal studies provided. Treat each personal study like a devotional and use them in whatever way works best for your schedule. You could do a partial section each day or complete the personal study all in one sitting. These personal studies are not intended to be burdensome or time-consuming but to provide a richer personal connection to the material and the concept Sarah dives into each video session.

SCHEDULE
SESSION ①

GROUP MEETING	**WATCH VIDEO SESSION 1** **GROUP DISCUSSION**
DAY ①	PERSONAL STUDY SESSION 1 **My Weakness Does Not Define Me**
DAY ②	PERSONAL STUDY SESSION 1 **Blotting Out My Transgressions**
DAY ③	PERSONAL STUDY SESSION 1 **What God Says About Me**
DAYS ④ – ⑤	READ INTRODUCTION, CHAPTERS 1–2 *Woman Evolve* book

DROP
THOSE
FIG LEAVES

What would happen if you were
willing to stand naked and
unashamed
before God?

WELCOME!

(2) MINUTES

Welcome to Session One of *Woman Evolve*. If this is your first time together as a group, take a moment to introduce yourselves to one another before watching the video. Then, let's get started!

OPENING DISCUSSION

(5) – (10) MINUTES

Answer the following questions to prepare for this week's video teaching:

If you've read or heard the story of Eve in the opening of Genesis, what's the first thing that comes to mind when you think of Eve?

Imagine yourself as the first woman on the earth. What would be the best thing and the most challenging thing about it?

SESSION ONE VIDEO

(21) MINUTES

Leader: *Play the video streaming or using the DVD. Each session opens with a dialogue between Sarah and a couple of friends. The teaching lesson follows just after each short conversation. Instruct your group to use the outline to follow along or take additional notes on anything that stands out.*

VIDEO NOTES

As you watch, take notes on anything that stands out to you.

- It's so much easier to stay put together than to bear it all.

- There's no feeling or trauma in your past that God hasn't already seen.

- God doesn't take a temporary moment and put it into your permanent record.

- Too often we rehearse failure when we should claim restoration.

- God says, *I can deal with your truth.*

- You have permission to not be okay, but to still be in the fight.

GROUP DISCUSSION
(45) MINUTES

Leader: *Read each numbered prompt and question to the group.*

1. What part of the teaching had the most impact on you? Take turns sharing with the group.

Sarah shares,

> "When we go into the hair salon,
> this is the **place** where all of our **truth**
> is **coming to the surface.**"

2. What is it about going to a salon that inspires you to become vulnerable? If not a salon, what is your place of secure vulnerability and what makes it safe?

Turn to Genesis 3:1–8, and let's have a few volunteers read the verses aloud, changing readers every few verses. Pay attention to what Adam and Eve do to protect themselves after they eat the forbidden fruit.

3. Reflecting on the story of the serpent, Adam, and Eve, who told you that you were naked? What was it in your life that told you God somehow made a mistake in His creation of you? Do you trust that God can cover you? Why or why not?

4. What kinds of "fig leaves" have you sewn together to hide what's really going on in your life? (Examples: looking good, working out, staying busy, etc.)

Sarah teaches that what we see and what God sees when we're naked are two different things. We see nakedness as our mistakes, fears, and insecurities on display, but that's not what God sees.

> "Before I formed you in the womb I knew you;
> Before you were born I sanctified you;
> I ordainewd you a prophet to the nations."
>
> **JEREMIAH 1:5**

God is more interested in preserving the memory of what He created than what you became to survive. And the more naked you become before God, the more you look like what God formed in your mother's womb.

5. What's an area of your life where you continue repeating a cycle, that, like Eve, ends with feeling less valuable or needing to hide? And how can you break this cycle?

6. Turn to Isaiah 43:25 and 1 John 1:9, and let's have someone different read each verse aloud. What do these verses reveal about the way God sees you and your sin?

7. Sarah tells the story of Ruth and Naomi. After so much loss, Naomi called herself Mara, meaning bitter, because her life was so hard (Ruth 1:20). Describe a time that made you feel like you should call yourself Mara. How did God demonstrate His grace, love, and kindness to you in that season?

Sarah teaches,

"We live in the place of **our strength** because
it is **easier than** dealing with the fragility of
our **weakness.** Yet in this sacred space that we're
creating, we're going to **stand boldly in our
weakness,** and we're going to do so by remembering
that our **weakness does not make us
weak,** that our **weakness does not
define us.** That is the place that God wants to
meet so that He can bring us to a
place of greater strength."

8. What fig leaves do you need to let go of so God can work His redeeming, restoring power in you?

CLOSING ACTIVITY
(5) MINUTES

1. Briefly review the video outline and any notes you took.

2. In the space below, write down the most significant thing you gained in this session—from the teaching or discussions.

   What I want to remember from this session is . . .

CLOSING PRAYER TIME

(4) MINUTES

Write a personal prayer here that reflects which area of this session's teaching you feel most in need of prayer.

Father God,

GROUP PRAYER

Leader: *Read this prayer aloud over the group.*

Forgive us for the areas where we've been hiding our pain and the truth from You. Forgive us for the ways we've sewn our own fig leaves and hid in the bushes instead of letting Your love cover us. Today, we drop the fig leaves. We stand before You naked and vulnerable, and ask for Your full restoration, Your full healing, Your full presence, and Your full power to make us whole. Help us to see ourselves and others the way You see us. In Jesus' name, Amen.

Leader: *Read these instructions about Personal Study between meetings to the group before dismissal.*

Every session in *Woman Evolve* includes three days of personal study and two days of reading to help you make meaningful connections between your life and what you're learning each week. In this first week, you'll work with the material in the **introduction** and **chapters 1 and 2 of the book Woman Evolve.**

PERSONAL STUDY

DAY 1
MY WEAKNESS DOES NOT DEFINE ME

Every day we're given opportunities to choose what we know is good and right for us. But if you're like me, there are times throughout the day when my desire to do what I know is good and right is overshadowed by the temptation to do what I know will ultimately slow my progress. In other words, I *know* what's better, but I don't *do* what's better.

The story of Eve in the book of Genesis reminds us that we're not alone in this battle. Now, for years I rolled my eyes whenever someone brought up Eve's name. I saw her as the woman who had *one* job and failed. But now I see Eve completely differently.

1. Have you tried to distance yourself from Eve in your mind and spirit? To somehow put space between yourself and the burden of being her daughter? In what ways? Why?

2. Which of the following words best describes what comes to your mind when you think about Eve? Circle all that apply.

Sin	Weak	Beautiful	Labor Pain
Mother	Cursed	Naive	Life
Insecurity	Doubting	Power Hungry	Beloved
Original Woman	Made from Man	The First	Sad
Shame	Fear	Regret	SecondChances
Wife	Betrayed	Defenseless	Willing

We're going to refer back to the story of Eve a lot throughout this study, but for now, let's focus on what got the best of her.

Read Genesis 3:1–6.

What did Eve know better than to do?

Who told her the rules?

Who *didn't* tell her the rules directly?

What did she do anyway?

3. Consider why the serpent chose Eve over Adam when the two of them were together in the garden. Adam was given instruction directly from God, but Eve heard of God's command secondhand. How might this secondhand hearing of God's command have left Eve more vulnerable to the serpent's lies than Adam?

4. Consider whether you are hearing directly from God or someone's secondhand delivery of God's Word and how might that be leaving you vulnerable to lies like Eve. Where are you vulnerable to lies in your life today?

5. What's one thing you knew better than to do today (or this week) but you did it anyway?

6. Which of the following do you tend to overdo, but you know better? Place a check mark (✔) next to the ones that tempt you.

_____ Tell little lies to make it through the day

_____ Overindulge and buy things you don't need

_____ Stalk the social media pages of those who hurt you

_____ Closet eat french fries in the car before you have dinner with everyone

_____ Overshare, meaning gossip, because it makes you feel like you're "in the know"

_____ Ghost someone online or around town because you don't want to have the honest, hard conversation

_____ Overspend your time, your commitments, your money

_____ Secretly eat your kids' candy stash

7. What do your temptations have in common with the temptations Eve faced in the garden?

8. What comfort do you find in knowing you're not the only one who is tempted or has given into temptation?

Read 1 Corinthians 10:13.

9. What promise does God make to you regarding temptation?

"You know what it's like to know better but not
do better . . . allowing our thoughts of shame,
anger, fear, anxiety, insecurity, and doubt to take
the mic—sometimes to the point we no longer
have the faith required to live life with integrity
or confidence." —from *Woman Evolve*, p. 4

10. What's an area of sin where you've allowed shame, anger, fear, or insecurity to fester?

11. Have you asked God to forgive you for your sin?

12. What do the following verses reveal about the forgiveness of sin?

Isaiah 55:7:

Proverbs 28:13:

James 5:15:

Acts 3:19:

1 John 1:9:

Eve confessed her disobedience to God, she got honest, she got naked, and God met her there. And if God did that for Eve, how much more does God want to do that for you and me?

I want you to see so much more in Eve than her mistake or her guilt. I want you to see her innocence, her strength, and how much courage she exhibited when she chose to be an active participant in her restoration process. She was not just the woman who ate from the forbidden fruit; she was the woman who paved the way for the ultimate Redeemer who would offer salvation to all humanity.

DAY 2
BLOTTING OUT MY TRANSGRESSIONS

Ever noticed how easy it is to get distracted from what you're called and created to do? Eve was the first to experience this in life. The serpent in the garden wasn't after Eve's appetite. The slithery, sneaky creature was after what she trusted as God's vision for her life. God's power in her life began to dissolve the moment she started questioning God's plan for her life.

1. Read Genesis 2:16–17. What does God specifically command regarding the tree of knowledge of good and evil?

2. Read Genesis 3:1. How does the serpent twist what God said?

3. Read Genesis 3:2–3. How does Eve twist or add to what God said in Genesis 2:16–17?

4. Read Genesis 3:4–5. How does the serpent twist what God said about eating from the tree of knowledge of good and evil?

The dialogue teaches us that uprooting the truth comes in a variety of ways. Sometimes an untruth is *added* to the truth. Sometimes partial truth is *subtracted* from the truth. And sometimes the truth is *twisted* or *turned upside down*. The result of all of these is untruth.

Yet, for Eve it all began with one question. A single question invaded Eve's mind, opened the floodgates, and changed her path:

> ## "Did God really say, 'You must not eat from any tree in the garden?'"
> ### GENESIS 3:1 (NIV)

That's all it took to suck Eve into questioning herself and the power, purpose, and potential God granted her. Look at what the question begins with: "Did God really say?"

5. Where in your life have you been tempted to think, "Did God really say?"

"The moment the woman's truth was uprooted and replaced with inquisition is the moment humanity took a sharp turn." —from *Woman Evolve*, p. 15

6. When was the first time your truth was uprooted?

7. When was the first time you no longer felt safe? Loved? Wanted? Liked? Good enough? Beautiful? Innocent?

8. How did that experience make you question God, yourself, and others?

"The serpent in the garden wasn't after Eve's appetite. He was after what she trusted as God's vision for her life." —from *Woman Evolve*, p. 15

9. What's eroding your trust in God?

10. How can you rise up and fight to place your full trust in God again?

11. Where do you most need to rise up and fight for God's vision for your life?

DAY ❸
WHAT GOD SAYS ABOUT ME

No one ends up stagnant in life because they want to be. We end up stagnant in life because the unknown is scary. Subconsciously, we believe that choosing to live in a perpetual state of indecision is better than making the wrong decision.

It's easy to move quickly when you aren't burdened down, but when you are heavy, you can't move as quickly. More than anything, what weighs us down internally are the thoughts that our fear, shame, past, and insecurities create.

If we could peek inside the mind of a person experiencing indecision, we would see that, generally, they aren't suffering from a lack of vision but rather the cloudiness that comes with playing out too many potential outcomes of that vision. Eventually everything becomes cloudy, and they lose the passion, creativity, and precision necessary to activate their next step.

1. On the continuum below, mark how much you feel stuck in life.

— ❶ — ❷ — ❸ — ❹ — ❺ — ❻ — ❼ — ❽ — ❾ — ❿ —

I'm moving
forward at a
healthy pace

I'm paralyzed
and don't
know what
to do

2. When you're feeling stuck, which of the following questions do you tend to struggle with most? Mark all that apply.

_____ Will it be worth it?   _____ Do I have what it takes?

_____ Can I get it done?   _____ Do I take a risk or play it safe?

_____ Do I stay or do I go?   _____ Do I try again and face
disappointment?

"The whirlwind of thoughts often blinds us from recognizing that they really have only two origins: they are birthed either from our faith or from our fear. Our fears pretend to keep us safe. Our faith demands we draw on courage we aren't sure we possess." —from *Woman Evolve*, p. 21

In Day Two's session, we looked at the question the cunning serpent asked Eve. What's interesting, if you re-read Genesis 3:1, you'll notice the serpent used the woman's mind against her. One of the greatest enemies lies between your ears and that's your thought-life. What you think will either help you become wiser, more compassionate, focused, and disciplined, or it will derail you, disempower you, and convince you that you don't have a chance—at anything.

3. What do the following verses reveal about your thoughts and mind?

SCRIPTURE	What the verse reveals about your thoughts and mind
ISAIAH 26:3	
ROMANS 12:1–2	

33

SCRIPTURE	What the verse reveals about your thoughts and mind
2 CORINTHIANS 10:3-6	
JAMES 1:8	
COLOSSIANS 3:1–2	
PHILIPPIANS 4:8	

4. What are you most tempted to believe that's untrue in each of the following areas?

Your relationship with God:

Your family:

Your past:

Your future:

5. How do the verses you looked up empower you to rise above these lies and false beliefs?

One of the biggest lies and false beliefs the serpent wanted to tempt Eve with is the same one he tempts us with today: God is not good.

6. In what area of your life have you been most tempted to believe that God is not good?

7. What do you do when experiences make you question whether God is good?

8. What do the following verses reveal about God's goodness?

Exodus 34:6:

Psalm 27:13:

Psalm 145:9:

9. Which is the most meaningful to you right now? Why?

SCHEDULE
SESSION ②

GROUP MEETING	**WATCH VIDEO SESSION 2** **GROUP DISCUSSION**
DAY ❶	PERSONAL STUDY SESSION 2 **God Wants to Heal Me**
DAY ❷	PERSONAL STUDY SESSION 2 **God Is Doing Something New in Me**
DAY ❸	PERSONAL STUDY SESSION 2 **I'm Taking that Step of Faith**
DAYS ❹ – ❺	READ CHAPTERS 3–4 *Woman Evolve* book

SESSION

DAMAGE
CONTROL

What if God
has a plan to heal
your deepest pain?

WELCOME!

Welcome to Session Two of *Woman Evolve*. If anyone is new to the group, take a moment to introduce yourselves to one another. Now, let's get started!

OPENING DISCUSSION

Answer the following questions to prepare for this week's video teaching:

When have you done something with your hair that you deeply regretted?

How did you respond and repair the situation?

SESSION TWO VIDEO

Leader: *Play the video streaming or using the DVD.*

VIDEO NOTES

As you watch, take notes on anything that stands out to you.

- You need deep conditioning

- Damage control is about finding a path to move forward

- The Spirit of God hovered over the face of the deep

- God gives us wisdom that we don't know we'll need

- The stone was a sign

- Damage control means we do the work of taking back the narrative

GROUP DISCUSSION

45 MINUTES

Leader: *Read each numbered prompt and question to the group.*

1. What part of the teaching had the most impact on you? Take turns sharing with the group.

2. When you think about damage and pain points in your past, do you tend to want God to do a quick fix or wait for His grace to deep condition those aching areas? Why?

3. When you think about those painful places, what are the go-to cover-ups you turn to rather than dealing with the actual damage? (Examples: achievement, perfection, avoiding tough conversations, isolation, drugs, sex, addiction.) How are these cover-ups affecting you? Your relationship with God? Your relationship with others?

Sarah shares,

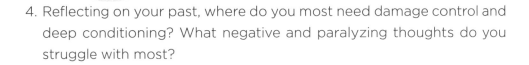

"When we **open** our **hearts**
for **damage control**, we start to face the
pain and find a deep **conditioning**
that comes from relationship with God.
We begin to break free from **negative**
and **paralyzing** thoughts like: **It's always**
going to be this way.
No one's ever going to love me.
No one could ever accept my past.
I'm never going to dream again."

4. Reflecting on your past, where do you most need damage control and deep conditioning? What negative and paralyzing thoughts do you struggle with most?

Turn to Joshua 4:1-9 and let's have a few volunteers read the verses aloud, changing readers every few verses. Pay attention to how God is preparing the children of Israel for what they'll face.

5. What's one stone of God's faithfulness in your life? Where have you become so comfortable in life, your Promised Land, that you've forgotten the cost and miracles that have allowed you to exist there?

6. Turn to Genesis 3:16, 20–24, and let's have someone read these verses aloud. After Eve eats the forbidden fruit, how does God help Eve with damage control and deep conditioning? Where do you see signs of God's grace, love, and protection in these verses?

Sarah teaches,

"You have an **opportunity** to do the
damage control with the Holy Spirit,
hovering over those deep spaces and
to **invite** God's presence (Genesis 1:2).
You're invited to go deeper—to not just stand
before God **naked** and **vulnerable**, but to
stand before God **hungry** for a **new way** of being.
From that place of hunger, you will be **fruitful**,
and you will **multiply**—
not because you did everything the right way,
but because you **partnered** with a **God**
who knows how to take you into the Promised Land."

7. Where do you sense God calling you deeper? What deeper work do you sense God wants to do in you?

8. Turn to Psalm 42:7, and let's have one person read the verse aloud. What prevents you from allowing God to do His deeper work in your life? What's one practical way you can move beyond this limitation and allow God to deep condition your heart this week?

CLOSING ACTIVITY

1. Briefly review the video outline and any notes you took.

2. In the space below, write down the most significant thing you gained in this session—from the teaching or discussions.

   What I want to remember from this session is . . .

CLOSING PRAYER TIME

 ④ MINUTES

Write a personal prayer that reflects which area of this session's teaching you feel most in need of prayer about.

Father God,

GROUP PRAYER

Leader: *Read this prayer aloud over the group.*

> Holy Spirit, I ask You to hover over my deepest areas of pain. Reveal the damage that my insecurities, fears, and shame have had on my mind, attitude, and thoughts. I ask You to deeply condition me in God's love, healing, power, and presence. Today, I give all of who I am to all of who You are. Help me to walk in the fullness of who You've made me to be. In Jesus' name, Amen.

Leader: *Read these instructions about Personal Study between meetings to the group before dismissal.*

Every session in *Woman Evolve* includes three days of personal study and two days of reading to help you make meaningful connections between your life and what you're learning each week. In this second week, you'll work with the material in **chapters 2 and 3 of the book *Woman Evolve.***

BETWEEN SESSIONS

PERSONAL STUDY

DAY 1
GOD WANTS TO HEAL ME

We need to explore the thoughts that environments of hurt produced in your life, as well as where you began to question God's goodness, your goodness, and the goodness of this world. The easiest, and scariest, place we will venture is the place in our history where we first experienced an unsettling disappointment.

1. What are the top three incidents from your past that still hurt or haunt you?

   #1:

   #2:

   #3:

2. How has each of these affected your emotions, thoughts, and how you feel about yourself? (Examples: Afraid, ashamed, devalued, weak, invisible, anxious.)

   #1:

   #2:

   #3:

3. When you think back on those three incidents, what's the hidden question that destabilized you in the first place? What underlying question has your soul been trying to answer? (Examples: Do I really matter? Does anyone love me? Will it ever be safe? Do I have value? Am I worthless?)

#1:

#2:

#3:

4. Now, ask yourself one simple question: What did you need to know in that moment or period of life? (Examples: I needed to know I was safe. I needed to know I wasn't alone. I needed to know I was loved. I needed to know that it was okay to still have hope.)

#1:

#2:

#3:

Sarah said, "For me, I really needed to know that I belonged. There was no limit to how far I was willing to go to finally put that question to rest. Though I believed my actions were my own, they were being fueled by the ache of questioning whether I belonged. I clung to any friendship, relationship, or opportunity that appeared to have the answer to that question. If I didn't fit into those friendships, relationships, or opportunities by being myself, I invented a version of me who could fit. That one question altered my thoughts and then those thoughts affected my actions."

5. Reflecting on the three incidents, the hidden questions, and what you've really needed to know, what's the question(s) driving you that you're ready to put to rest?

Read Jeremiah 29:11.

6. Do you believe God's plans are bigger and better than the question(s) driving you? Why or why not?

7. Take a moment and place your question(s) before God. Ask the Holy Spirit how He wants to answer your question. Pay attention to any scriptures that may come to mind. Write your response below:

DAY 2
GOD IS DOING SOMETHING NEW IN ME

Let's return to the story of Eve where we first began. Once Adam and Eve eat the forbidden fruit, God calls to them. The response of Adam and Eve couldn't be more different.

Read Genesis 3:9–13.

1. How does Adam respond to God?

2. How does Eve respond to God?

3. What surprises you about their responses?

4. Who is more honest?

5. Who plays the victim card and therefore blames their actions on the other?

6. When have you done something you regretted and used blame as a form of self-defense? What was the outcome?

One of the great lessons and gifts Eve gave us is that if you're willing to be honest and vulnerable, there's no amount of damage to your spirit that is irreparable. What was done cannot be undone, but nothing is beyond God's redemption.

Read Genesis 3:20.

7. What good was God going to work through Eve, no matter what?

Read Romans 8:28.

8. When have you seen something that didn't start as good end up producing good because of God's faithfulness?

9. What's one area where you've given up on God bringing about good?

10. What do the following verses reveal about how God is doing a new work and bringing about good? Fill in the chart below.

SCRIPTURE	How the verse reveals God doing a new work and bringing about good
GENESIS 50:20	
ISAIAH 43:18–19	

SCRIPTURE	How the verse reveals God doing a new work and bringing about good
LAMENTATIONS 3:22–24	
2 CORINTHIANS 4:16–17	

11. Which verses are most meaningful to you now? Why?

12. In the space below, write those verses as a personal prayer for God to do a new work in you.

DAY 3
I'M TAKING THAT STEP OF FAITH

God's presence can stop the flow of any damage you've experienced, but you'll have to be intentional about inviting God to do His work in you. One of the places we see this demonstrated is in the book of Joshua.

When the Israelites are set free from Pharoah's wicked rule, they pack up to leave Egypt. They soon find themselves chased down by the Egyptian armies and pinned up against the Red Sea. God splits the sea in two and the Israelites safely make the crossing while the Egyptian armies are destroyed by the crashing waters. This crossing marks the Israelites' journey from slavery to freedom.

After forty years of wandering in the desert, the Israelites find themselves again at the edge of a great water crossing. This time, it's the Jordan River, and it's all that stands between them and the Promised Land. Now the Ark—God's presence—was carried in front of the people.

Read Joshua 3:1–5.

1. Why do you think Joshua commands the people to follow the Ark rather than lead the Ark?

2. Do you tend to try follow God into the unknown or tell God where He should take you? Explain.

Read Joshua 3:6.

3. What does Joshua tell the people?

4. On the continuum below, mark how much you're expectant of God to meet you, restore you, and set you free.

I don't
expect God
to work soon,
if at all

I live with
great hope
for God to
move mightily

Read Joshua 3:7–13.

5. What did the Ark, God's presence, do to stop the river?

6. In what ways have you been standing at the shore of God's presence and restoration rather than taking the step into God's presence and restoration?

Read Joshua 3:14–17.

7. What's the result of following Joshua's instruction?

8. What step of faith is God calling you to make to confront the damage from your past?

9. How does this story encourage you to make that step of faith?

SCHEDULE
SESSION ③

GROUP MEETING	**WATCH VIDEO SESSION 3** **GROUP DISCUSSION**
DAY ❶	PERSONAL STUDY SESSION 3 **It's Time to Overcome the Enemy**
DAY ❷	PERSONAL STUDY SESSION 3 **You're a Person, Not a Persona!**
DAY ❸	PERSONAL STUDY SESSION 3 **Let's Be Fruitful and Multiply**
DAYS ❹ – ❺	READ CHAPTERS 5–6 *Woman Evolve* book

SESSION ③

WHAT
ARE WE DOING
TODAY?

What if the setbacks, the disappointments, and the discouragements of life are the devil hiding in plain sight?

WELCOME!

 MINUTES

Welcome to Session Three of *Woman Evolve*. Take a moment to greet each other before watching the video. Then, let's get started!

OPENING DISCUSSION

 MINUTES

Answer the following questions to prepare for this week's video teaching:

When you read the news or hear terrible stories, how often do you think that it's evil or the enemy at work?

What evidence do you point to that suggests the devil is real?

SESSION THREE VIDEO

 MINUTES

Leader: *Play the video streaming or using the DVD.*

VIDEO NOTES

As you watch, take notes on anything that stands out to you.

- Purpose is found in how you show up to life

- It's what you're going to do and who you're becoming

- Jesus came to declare war on the other kingdoms

- God, give me an opportunity to bear light

- The real enemy is after that light

- Just because you graduate, don't burn the schoolhouse down

GROUP DISCUSSION
(45) MINUTES

Leader: *Read each numbered prompt and question to the group.*

1. What part of the teaching had the most impact on you? Take turns sharing with the group.

Sarah shares,

"Just as a hairdresser asks,
'What are we doing today?' we
face similar questions. In the in-between
stage of **disconnecting** from our **past**
and showing up fully in our **present**,
we must wrestle with some
tough questions."

2. Where do you most need to shed your old skin, break free from what's holding you back, or refuse to be afraid?

3. What's stopping you from disconnecting from your past? What do you think God wants to do with your present?

4. When you think about your life, how do you answer the following questions: "What do I want to do now?" and "Who do I want to be now?"

5. Turn to Ephesians 6:12, 1 Peter 5:8–9, and John 10:10, and let's have someone different read each verse or verses aloud. What do these verses reveal about the enemy and his mission? What do they reveal about what God's given you to overcome the enemy? What situations are you facing now where you're attributing cause to the wrong source and it's really the enemy you're wrestling with?

Sarah teaches,

> "When Jesus comes to Peter and
> Andrew fishing, He says, '**Follow me,**
> and I will make you **fishers of men.'**
> **(Matthew 4:19)**
> In essence, Jesus says, 'I'm going to **use**
> what you **already know** how to do but
> **show you** how to use it and what
> I'm doing to establish my **kingdom.'**
> Jesus takes what the disciples
> understood, and that **leads** them into their **destiny.**
> God wastes nothing."

6. What's one gift or talent you've been overlooking that God wants to use? How can you use your gifts, your talents, and your struggles to magnify God's kingdom?

7. Turn to Matthew 5:14 and let's have someone different read the verse aloud. How does living in the light mean there's nowhere for the enemy to have victory? Why is living in the light of Jesus, naked and unashamed, the best way to live?

8. Turn to Ephesians 5:8 and let's have someone different read the verse aloud. What new opportunities has God given you to be a light-bearer? How has God established you as a flame that cannot be extinguished? How is the light in you helping and freeing others?

CLOSING ACTIVITY
 MINUTES

1. Briefly review the video outline and any notes you took.

2. In the space below, write down the most significant thing you gained in this session—from the teaching or discussions.

   What I want to remember from this session is . . .

CLOSING PRAYER TIME
(4) MINUTES

Write a personal prayer that reflects which area of this session's teaching you feel most in need of prayer.

Father God,

GROUP PRAYER

Leader: *Read this prayer aloud over the group.*

> I want to light up this world with You. Expose any areas of darkness in me. I want to live in Your light and shine Your light everywhere I go. Through Your power, help me overcome every attack of the enemy and rise victorious. Help me to step out boldly and help set others free. In Jesus' name, Amen.

Leader: *Read these instructions about Personal Study between meetings to the group before dismissal.*

Every session in *Woman Evolve* includes three days of personal study and two days of reading to help you make meaningful connections between your life and what you're learning each week. In this third week, you'll work with the material in **chapters 5 and 6 of the book *Woman Evolve.***

BETWEEN SESSIONS
PERSONAL STUDY

DAY 1
IT'S TIME TO OVERCOME THE ENEMY

It's easier to stand up to a devil you can see than it is to fight the one that hides in plain sight. We see the power of hate, wickedness, and darkness every single day. It's plastered on the news, with stories of senseless violence, acts of terrorism, and schemes rooted in greed.

I'm no longer asking God to exclusively grant us wisdom, strategy, and grace for the evil we see. I'm asking God to make me aware of what is in my heart, home, or community that is at war with my ability to partner with God in bringing the world to its greatest potential. I don't know where the devils I can't see are hiding, so I have to be intentional about making sure I'm postured to defeat any negative paradigm or thought that dares to dilute the power God has given me to effect change.

Read Ephesians 6:10–18.

1. In the space below, draw a picture of the armor of God and note what each part does.

2. How do the various pieces of the armor work together to protect you and empower you to overcome the enemy?

3. Which of the pieces of the armor of God are easiest for you to put on each day? Why?

4. Which of the pieces of the armor of God are hardest for you to put on each day? Why?

5. What prayers or practices can you employ to make sure you're armored-up each day?

6. What do the following verses reveal about the tools God gives you to overcome the enemy? Fill in the chart below.

SCRIPTURE	What the verse reveals about the tools God gives you to help you overcome
1 CORINTHIANS 15:57	
HEBREWS 7:25	
1 JOHN 3:9	
1 JOHN 5:4	
REVELATION 12:11	

7. Which of these verses do you most need to commit to memory? Why?

8. Which of these strategies do you most need to employ now?

DAY ②
YOU'RE A PERSON, NOT A PERSONA!

God was walking in the cool of the garden looking for Adam and Eve when they began to hide. God called out for them, and Adam spoke up, telling God that when they heard God's voice they hid because they were naked. God responded in Genesis 3:11, "Who told you that you were naked? Have you eaten from the tree of which I commanded you that you should not eat?"

Let's dissect the character of God in this instance. He didn't berate the man or the woman, nor did He shame them. God gave them space to present the truth as they knew it.

1. Look up the following verses and fill in the chart below.

SCRIPTURE	What characteristics of God appear in the verse?
PSALM 18:30	
ISAIAH 40:28	

SCRIPTURE	What characteristics of God appear in the verse?
JAMES 1:17	
1 TIMOTHY 1:17	
2 PETER 3:9	
1 JOHN 5:3	

2. Reflecting on the chart above, which of these characteristics of God are demonstrated in His response to Adam and Eve in the garden?

3. Which of the characteristics of God listed in the chart above have you experienced personally?

4. If God didn't shame Adam and Eve, then why are we so tempted to shame each other?

God knew in that moment that the man and the woman were bearing fruit, but it wasn't the type of fruit God intended for them. When you know how good and holy and loving God is, you have no need to hide your raw, naked vulnerability from Him. We only begin to hide when we no longer trust who He is.

Don't fall into the trap of only presenting your good parts to God. You're a person, not a persona. It's much easier to present a persona to God than to present a person, but God doesn't want who you pretend to be.

5. Do you tend to present your person to God or your persona? Explain.

Read 1 Chronicles 16:34 and Psalm 36:7.

6. What do these verses reveal about how much God wants to scoop you up in His love just as you are?

DAY ③
LET'S BE FRUITFUL AND MULTIPLY

When God was in the garden He blessed creation, then told the first couple to be fruitful and multiply, but I don't think He was just talking about having sex and making babies. God was preparing humanity to live in a perpetual state of production where we are to take what God has given us, plant it, and allow it to produce over and over again.

When the serpent invaded Eve's realm and convinced her to eat from the tree, that snake was manipulating God's formula to fit his agenda. The serpent had a plan for the woman to be fruitful and multiply, but this time the fruit wouldn't make the world better. This time the fruit would separate humanity from God's vision.

The moment the woman ate from the tree, the serpent's idea was fruitful. But the moment God cursed the serpent in Genesis 3:15, that bad fruit was in jeopardy of no longer being able to multiply.

Let me quickly break this down for you: It doesn't matter what seed has been fruitful in your life. Your family may have been producing the type of fruit that has caused dysfunction for generations, but it is never too late to root out the bad seeds and plant God's seeds in their place.

Read Galatians 5:22–23.

1. In the chart on the next page, make a list of the facets of the fruit of the Spirit. Next to each one, place an (**X**) indicating whether you see each one growing, stagnating, or shrinking in your life.

FRUIT	GROWING	STAGNATING	SHRINKING

2. What does this reveal about how you're really doing spiritually?

3. How does this compare to the plans and purposes God has for you?

4. What changes do you need to make to allow the fruit of the Spirit to grow in you?

5. Look up each of the following verses. What does each one reveal about the fruit God wants to grow in you?

Matthew 3:8:

John 15:8:

John 15:16:

John 15:5:

James 3:18:

6. Which one of these do you desire most in your life? Why?

7. Write a prayer in the space below asking God to produce that fruit in you.

SCHEDULE
SESSION ④

GROUP MEETING	**WATCH VIDEO SESSION 4** **GROUP DISCUSSION**
DAY ①	PERSONAL STUDY SESSION 4 **No More Strife in My Life**
DAY ②	PERSONAL STUDY SESSION 4 **I Can't Be All Things to All People**
DAY ③	PERSONAL STUDY SESSION 4 **Prayer Is Mighty Powerful**
DAYS ④ – ⑤	READ CHAPTERS 7–8 *Woman Evolve* book

SESSION

YOU
NEED A
TRIM

What if boundaries
are the missing ingredient for your
breakthrough?

WELCOME!

Ⓒ MINUTES

Welcome to Session Four of *Woman Evolve*. Take a moment for group members to connect before watching the video. Then, let's get started!

OPENING DISCUSSION

⑤ – ⑩ MINUTES

Answer the following questions to prepare for this week's video teaching:

Much like trimming your hair, establishing healthy boundaries is necessary for a healthy life. What's one healthy boundary that you've set for yourself that's worked well?

What's one area where you didn't set a healthy boundary and now you wish you had?

SESSION FOUR VIDEO

㉑ MINUTES

Leader: *Play the video streaming or using the DVD.*

VIDEO NOTES

As you watch, take notes on anything that stands out to you.

⊚ When God created the heavens and earth, everything had a boundary

⊚ Boundaries protect the work God is doing in your life

⊚ When you step out in faith, you've got to protect the abundance

⊚ Don't let your faith be diluted by someone else's disbelief

⊚ Jesus built His church on Peter—a man who tried to tell Jesus not to go to the cross

GROUP DISCUSSION

(45) MINUTES

Leader: *Read each numbered prompt and question to the group.*

1. What part of the teaching had the most impact on you? Take turns sharing with the group.

Sarah shares,

"I want you to **begin** preparing your
friendships, your **churches**, and your
community for this new version of who you are.
Not in a way that is prideful or boastful, but in
a way that says, I **need** something **different**
than I needed before. I need you to **stop**
doting on me and instead
begin cheering me on in what
God has for me."

2. Are you surrounding yourself with people who cheer you on in your growth, transformation, and evolution, or with people who hold you back from God's greater work? Explain. What boundaries do you need to set so your friends can become people who champion your growth in Jesus?

Turn to Genesis 13:1–11, and let's have a few volunteers read the verses aloud, changing readers every few verses. Pay attention to the healthy boundaries Abram draws to protect the relationship.

3. What healthy boundaries does Abram establish with Lot? Who is your Lot?

4. What's one relationship where you've become entangled and need to disentangle so the relationship can become healthier? What's the healthy boundary you need to draw so you don't become bitter?

5. Sarah teaches that your faith can be diluted by someone else's disbelief. The herders of Abram and Lot were beginning to have strife and quarrel. A war was developing. In their situation, a lack of boundaries can devour your energy, creativity, time, and resources. What's the high cost of low or no boundaries for you relationally? Spiritually? Financially? For your future?

Turn to Matthew 16:13–23, and let's have a few volunteers read the verses aloud, changing readers every few verses. Pay attention to Peter's changing response to Jesus fulfilling what He's come to do.

6. How does Peter go from celebrating Jesus' purpose to trying to block Jesus' purpose? Who once celebrated you, but now is holding you back from your God-given purpose?

7. What's the hardest part about drawing healthy boundaries? What are three best practices you've found for setting healthy boundaries? How can setting boundaries become the seeds for revival in your life and those around you?

Sarah shares,

> "Sometimes our time with God
> becomes an **afterthought**.
> It's something we **check off** at the end of the day,
> or we think because we're **serving**
> the way that **everyone else** does we've
> done our **part** for God. But **serving**
> God is not the same as **receiving** from God.
> Jesus found a way to be more
> **intentional** about **protecting** what
> God wanted to do **through Him** than protecting
> the **comfort** of those around Him."

8. What healthy boundaries are you drawing around your relationship and time with God? What changes do you need to make for your relationship with God to flourish?

CLOSING ACTIVITY

 MINUTES

1. Briefly review the video outline and any notes you took.

2. In the space below, write down the most significant thing you gained in this session—from the teaching or discussions.

   What I want to remember from this session is . . .

CLOSING PRAYER TIME

④ MINUTES

Write a personal prayer that reflects which area of this session's teaching you feel most in need of prayer.

Father God,

GROUP PRAYER

Leader: *Read this prayer aloud over the group.*

> Give me the wisdom, strength, and grace to draw healthy boundaries around my relationship with You and with others. Help me identify the people who are pulling me away from the abundance You have for me. Provide strategies on how to disentangle well, and help me draw boundaries that keep me away from temptation. Help me protect the environment where You want to produce a miracle. In Jesus' name, Amen.

Leader: *Read these instructions about Personal Study between meetings to the group before dismissal.*

Every session in *Woman Evolve* includes three days of personal study and two days of reading to help you make meaningful connections between your life and what you're learning each week. In this fourth week, you'll work with the material **in chapters 7 and 8 of the book *Woman Evolve.***

BETWEEN SESSIONS

PERSONAL STUDY

DAY

NO MORE STRIFE IN MY LIFE

Just like trimming hair is necessary to remove split ends, we need to draw boundaries in our lives to remove the things that are diluting our faith and drawing us away from God. Let's revisit the story of Abram and Lot.

Read Genesis 13:8–9.

1. What role did strife play in alerting Abram there was a problem?

2. Where are you experiencing strife in your life right now?

3. How does the strife signal there's a problem that needs to be dealt with?

4. How does Abram demonstrate kindness and grace in the way he draws a healthy boundary with Lot?

5. When has someone drawn a healthy boundary with you and exhibited kindness and grace? What did you learn from that experience?

6. When you think about the strife in your life and the healthy boundaries you need to draw, what tactics or strategies can you implement from Abram's approach to Lot?

7. Read Genesis 13:10–13. How does Lot choosing the best land for himself compare to Abram sacrificially giving Lot first choice?

8. When have you been generous and the recipient responded with selfishness? How did you handle the situation?

9. Read Genesis 13:14–17. How does God reward Abram even though he was left with the least amount of land?

10. Describe a time when it looked like you were taken advantage of, but God showed Himself good. What did you learn about God through that experience?

DAY 2
I CAN'T BE ALL THINGS TO ALL PEOPLE

God wants to set up each life to multiply. If you're constantly living divided, depleted, and depressed, then multiplication is out of reach. This is not about doing nothing for anyone, but it is an opportunity to be honest about where your limits are and to know when you've gone from being like Jesus to becoming someone's savior.

1. Where do you struggle to set limits for yourself?

2. Where have you bought into the lie that you can be all things for all people?

3. Where are you most tempted to be the savior rather than allowing Jesus to be the Savior?

Read John 5:19-20.

4. How did Jesus tell the difference between what He could do and what God was telling Him to do?

5. How did Jesus resist the pressure of being everything to everyone?

6. What have you signed up for or volunteered to do that God never asked you to do?

7. How can you gently pull back to make space for the greater assignment God has for you?

DAY ③
PRAYER IS MIGHTY POWERFUL

Just like for Abram, your boundaries are not rooted in self-preservation or selfishness, but rather protecting what God is doing. A boundary is easier to maintain when it's connected to the development that is taking place in your walk with the Lord. Gently letting someone know you don't have as much time for them as you'd like is hard, but when you know that boundary is allowing you to spend more time with God, helping you to overcome a depression, or allowing you to pour into your own cup, it makes a difference.

Though pressed with endless needs and demands, Jesus demonstrated the importance of retreating to spend time with God throughout His ministry.

Read Mark 1:35–38.

   1. What stands out to you about Jesus' time of solitude?

   2. Which of these practices do you need to incorporate in your life and relationship with God?

Read Mark 6:25–31.

   3. What compels Jesus to withdraw?

   4. What practices does Jesus call His disciples to in these verses?

   5. Which of these practices do you need to incorporate in your life and relationship with God?

6. What do the following verses reveal about Jesus' prayer life? Fill in the chart below.

SCRIPTURE	Details about Jesus' prayer life
MATTHEW 14:23	
LUKE 3:21	
LUKE 6:21	
LUKE 9:28–29	

Prayer is an opportunity to be reminded of who God is and to bring our hearts into alignment with His purpose and will. It's not just a moment when we ask for what we need, but rather an opportunity to present ourselves fully. While some people are anointed to pray effortlessly, others need some guidance on the best way to open their hearts and invite God's presence within them. There are four steps to open your heart in prayer.

#1: *Adoration.* No differently than when we meet someone and are inspired because of what they've done, adoration is an opportunity for us to recognize God's résumé. With His fullness in mind, words start coming to my mouth: "You are wonderful. You are majestic. You are a healer. You are a provider. You are perfect in all Your ways. You are all-knowing."

7. In the space below, write God's résumé and share your personal adoration of God for who He is and what He's done.

#2 Confession. Prayer is a safe place to admit where we've fallen short, especially in comparison to who God is. We can ask forgiveness for anything, from complaining and doubting to bitterness and frustration.

8. In the space below, confess what you've done and ask for God's forgiveness.

#3 Gratitude. No matter what you're facing, there's always things to be thankful for.

9. In the space below, write at least five things you're grateful for.

YOU NEED A TRIM

#4 Intercession. This is when our will and God's will begin to wrestle. We don't just ask for what we like or prefer, but for God to qualify our desires so His will is first. We do this for ourselves and others.

10. In the space below, write at least three names of people you know who need God's intervention and write at least one area where you're struggling with God's will.

Prayer is the one sure way to find release in every situation—whether with people or circumstances. Use it to help open your eyes to God's truth in your everyday life. Prayer changes everything—including you.

SCHEDULE
SESSION ⑤

GROUP MEETING	**WATCH VIDEO SESSION 5** **GROUP DISCUSSION**
DAY ❶	PERSONAL STUDY SESSION 5 **Make Space for Your Peace**
DAY ❷	PERSONAL STUDY SESSION 5 **You Need Your Goals**
DAY ❸	PERSONAL STUDY SESSION 5 **You Need to Overcome Setbacks**
DAYS ❹ — ❺	READ CHAPTERS 9–10 *Woman Evolve* book

SESSION

NO TURNING BACK

What if God's desire isn't
that you do everything perfectly,
but that you never
stop reaching for Him?

WELCOME!

 MINUTES

Welcome to Session Five of *Woman Evolve.* Take a moment to greet each other before watching the video. Then, let's get started!

OPENING DISCUSSION

 MINUTES

Answer the following questions to prepare for this week's video teaching:

What's one area where you've really changed or grown from who you once were?

Discuss any ways in which you fear going back to your previous self.

SESSION FIVE VIDEO

 MINUTES

Leader: *Play the video streaming or using the DVD.*

VIDEO NOTES

As you watch, take notes on anything that stands out to you.

- We are afraid of reverting

- Mary is a role model

- The secret sauce is in retracing your steps

- Never stop reaching

- Performance says if I can't do it well, I won't do it at all

- Your mind, thoughts, and heart need to reach for peace

GROUP DISCUSSION

(45) MINUTES

Leader: *Read each numbered prompt and question to the group.*

1. What part of the teaching had the most impact on you? Take turns sharing with the group.

Sarah shares,

"There are moments where we are **afraid** to establish **ourselves** in our new **truth**, our **new** way of being, because we are **afraid** of **reverting** or going back to those **same actions** and **behaviors** that landed us in the condition of needing to be transformed in the first place."

2. When you think about the progress you've made in your life, your faith, and your spiritual journey; where are you most afraid of reverting? How is your fear of failure keeping you from ownership of what God has for you now?

Turn to Luke 2:41–50, and let's have a few volunteers read the verses aloud, changing readers every few verses. Pay attention to how long Mary had to search for her son.

3. What emotions do you think Mary felt as a mother who lost her son, Jesus? When you've dropped the ball, forgotten something important, or really messed up, what emotions tend to flood you?

Sarah shares,

"In that **difficult** time, Mary reasons that even though she may have **lost Jesus** for a moment, she doesn't have to lose Jesus **permanently**. She goes back and **retraces** her steps. She goes back and **keeps looking** because at the end of the day, she's going to **complete** what God **sent her** on this earth to do. **Loss** has a way of making you **question** whether you're **fit** for the role, but loss **doesn't change** God's mind about you."

4. What assignment do you feel like God has given you? Where do you feel like you've lost your way or confidence in that assignment?

5. What does it look like for you to retrace your steps, remain faithful, and remember God's calling for you?

Turn to Philippians 3:12–14, and let's have a volunteer read the verses aloud. Pay attention to Paul's commitment to reach for Christ.

6. What does it look like for you to reach for God with everything you've got? What does it look like for you to reach for God amid everyday battles including depression, exhaustion, and grief? Where have you convinced yourself that God is no longer reaching for you?

Sarah teaches that performance tells us that if we can't do it well, then we shouldn't do it at all. But that's not God's plan for your life. Resisting the pressure to perform in your relationship with God is hard, but Jesus shows us how to keep our minds focused on God.

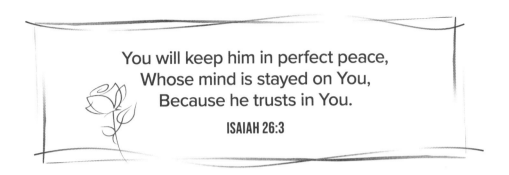

You will keep him in perfect peace,
Whose mind is stayed on You,
Because he trusts in You.

ISAIAH 26:3

7. Where are you most tempted by performance and perfection in life? In your relationship with God?

8. What are the little thieves that try to steal your peace? What changes do you need to make to experience Jesus as the Prince of Peace today?

CLOSING ACTIVITY

 MINUTES

1. Briefly review the video outline and any notes you took.

2. In the space below, write down the most significant thing you gained in this session—from the teaching or discussions.

   What I want to remember from this session is . . .

CLOSING PRAYER TIME

(4) MINUTES

Write a personal prayer that reflects which area of this session's teaching you feel most in need of prayer about.

Father God,

GROUP PRAYER

Leader: *Read this prayer aloud over the group.*

> God, I cling to Your promise that the good work You started in me will be brought to completion. I will not revert to my old ways, because You are always doing something new. Forgive me for turning to performance and perfection to try to gain the favor and grace You've so freely given. Fill me with Your peace, because You are the Prince of Peace and keep me faithful every day of my life. In Jesus' name, Amen.

Leader: *Read these instructions about Personal Study between meetings to the group before dismissal.*

Every session in *Woman Evolve* includes three days of personal study and two days of reading to help you make meaningful connections between your life and what you're learning each week. In this fifth week, you'll work with the material in **chapters 9 to 10 of the book *Woman Evolve.***

PERSONAL STUDY

DAY **1**
MAKE SPACE FOR YOUR PEACE

Sometimes in trying to focus on the comfort of others, we ignore the responsibility we have to ourselves. The career must be pursued. The home must be clean. The dinner must be cooked. The friends must be in place. The skin must be clear. The pressure is on to create a picture-perfect existence, with us as the photographer. The only problem is, we become so busy creating the picture that we never step into the frame. We can't just make space for every*one* and every*thing* else and ignore the fact that we take up space too. When we forget this, we will certainly lose our peace.

There's a moment in the Bible that speaks to this very thing. In Luke 10:38, Jesus visits two sisters, Martha and Mary. Martha wants to ensure the house is spick-and-span for Jesus. Imagine the pressure! While she's running around like a wild chicken getting everything done, she notices her sister, Mary, sitting idly by Jesus. Martha is my petty homegirl for this because instead of giving Mary that frustrated "girl, if you don't get up right now" look, she snitches on Mary to Jesus.

Read Luke 10:38–40.

1. What was Martha distracted by?

2. What activities tend to leave you feeling distracted and overwhelmed?

3. Why do you think Martha addresses Jesus instead of Mary with the concern?

4. When you have a complaint about someone not carrying their weight, do you tend to go to the person or other people?

Read Luke 10:41–42.

5. What does Jesus diagnose as what's really going on with Martha?

6. Where in your life are you struggling with the same things? How is this stealing your peace?

What's interesting about Jesus' statement is that He wasn't going to spend the rest of His time at the house with Martha and Mary. Soon He'd be heading to the next town. When He said that Mary had chosen that good part, "which will not be taken away from her," Jesus was not talking about His physical body. He was talking about what happens when we are in God's presence.

7. What does it look like for you to choose the "good part" with Jesus?

8. How does spending time with Jesus stay with you long after you've left that location?

9. When is the best time of day for you to engage in prayer or meditation so you can alleviate your worries and receive a steadiness that cannot be taken away from you?

10. How can you make this part of your daily life?

DAY **2**
YOU NEED YOUR GOALS

If you've come to a place where you've accepted your identity as an extension of God on earth, it may take some time for you to figure out exactly how you're supposed to show up and where you will be most effective. That means there may be moments when even your best efforts end in failure. Even when we fail in the pursuit of what God has for us, we have a promise that it will all work out for our good. One of the disciples who demonstrated this best is Peter.

Read Matthew 8:23–27.

1. Why were all the disciples so afraid? Would your response have been any different? Why or why not?

2. What declaration does Jesus make that brings them peace?

Read Matthew 16:13–19.

3. How does Peter's response to Jesus differ from the other disciples?

4. Where do you most need to hear the clear voice and instruction of God in your life?

5. What great storm is raging in your life right now?

6. Are you asking God to end the storm or allow you to walk through the storm? Explain.

7. What distracts Peter? What's distracting you from doing the thing God has called you to? How can you recenter your focus on Jesus again?

Peter set a goal of walking to Jesus. He didn't make it all the way, but he's still taken more steps on water than you or I ever have. I want you to begin making goals for yourself without fear of failure or of the unknown. I want you to come to a place where you are content with starting to head in the right direction and that you don't get caught up in whether you'll reach the desired destination—knowing that, like Peter, you're going to grow in faith in the process.

8. Take a moment to prayerfully reflect on three short-term and long-term goals.

SHORT-TERM GOALS	LONG-TERM GOALS

9. How might pursuing these goals change your life and your family for generations to come?

DAY ③
YOU NEED TO OVERCOME SETBACKS

Now when you set goals, sooner or later you're going to encounter setbacks. It may look like Peter, whose name means "Rock," sinking just like one. Or it may look much different. Let's talk about Eve. After the fall, this woman receives her name, meaning, "mother of all the living." But for Eve, that's more than a name, it's a goal, it's a mission, it's who she's called to become. She starts out on track, fulfilling her God-given goals and calling.

Read Genesis 4:1–2.

1. How is Eve fulfilling her goals and calling?

2. What's one goal you've set that you've seen forward momentum toward or reached?

3. What's one goal you've set that remains unmet or has become a place of pain?

For Eve, she had come into alignment with what God said her focus should be, and she started producing based on that place of alignment. The only problem is—and if you don't know how the story ends, this is going to be a major spoiler—Cain kills Abel.

Read Genesis 4:3–8.

4. What do you imagine this was like for Eve?

It seems like we should be able to go from: God spoke it, I obeyed it, and it came to pass, but anyone who has ever attempted to do anything that requires faith knows that often there are moments when the result doesn't look like what God said.

5. Where have you experienced this kind of disappointment or setback?

6. How did you respond?

Read Genesis 4:25–26.

7. How does Eve respond to her goal and calling even after severe loss and disappointment?

8. What is the fruit of her faithfulness and persistence? What inspires you most about what Eve did?

9. If one of the outcomes of your goals doesn't look like what you thought God had said, will you be bold enough to try again until something in your life looks like what God said? Why or why not?

10. When setting goals, why is it important to commit to the process and not just the outcome?

11. Reflecting on the list of goals in yesterday's homework, how do you
suspect God is going to use the process, not the outcome of your goals,
to grow and evolve you?

SCHEDULE
SESSION ⑥

GROUP MEETING	WATCH VIDEO SESSION 6 GROUP DISCUSSION
DAY ❶	PERSONAL STUDY SESSION 6 **The Best Friends for You**
DAY ❷	PERSONAL STUDY SESSION 6 **You're an Overcomer**
DAY ❸	PERSONAL STUDY SESSION 6 **Woman Evolve!**
DAYS ❹ – ❺	READ CHAPTER 11 *Woman Evolve* book

SESSION ⑥

DON'T
DO IT
ALONE

What if you lived
vulnerably and authentically
as part of a sisterhood of
believers?

WELCOME!

(2) MINUTES

Welcome to Session Six of *Woman Evolve*. Take a moment to greet each other before watching the video. Then, let's get started!

OPENING DISCUSSION

(5) – (10) MINUTES

Answer the following questions to prepare for this week's video teaching:

Name one person who champions you in your faith.

Name one person you champion in their faith.

SESSION SIX VIDEO

(23) MINUTES

Leader: *Play the video streaming or using the DVD.*

VIDEO NOTES

As you watch, take notes on anything that stands out to you.

- Vulnerability among women is a gateway for divine confirmation

- Comparing yourself to others

- Mary and Martha

- Ruth and Naomi

- You are somebody's hero, somebody's mentor in the making

- You can receive the companionship of others and Jesus

GROUP DISCUSSION
(45) MINUTES

Leader: *Read each numbered prompt and question to the group.*

1. What part of the teaching had the most impact on you? Take turns sharing with the group.

Sarah shares,

"**Vulnerability** is hard for us to experience ourselves, and experiencing it with **other women** is even more **challenging**. God loves when we **share** what He's doing in our life, because it **confirms** for another woman that **heartbreak** doesn't have to be the end, that **depression** doesn't have to have the final say, and that **anxiety** does not have to be your ruler. But we will never know this unless we are **willing** to come **together** in a place of **vulnerability**."

2. What holds you back from being more vulnerable with yourself? With other women?

3. Describe a time when you were encouraged and empowered because a woman of faith shared her story. Why are spiritual friendships so essential for spiritual growth?

Turn to Luke 10:38–42, and let's have a few volunteers read the verses aloud, changing readers every few verses. Pay attention to the role comparison plays in the story.

4. How does Martha compare herself to Mary? How does comparing yourself to others—for what they have or don't have—affect your ability to know and be known by others?

5. Who is one person you not only judged, but also compared yourself to, only to later find out you were dead wrong? What did you learn from that experience?

Sarah shares,

"When we begin to recognize that we
are **spiritually connected** to **every**
woman on the earth, it **changes** how we **show
up** in the world. We can **draw** on the
great cloud of **witnesses**—from Sarai to
Rahab. You can remember **spiritual heroes** and
so many who have gone before you and
shown you what's **possible**."

6. Who are your spiritual heroes in the Bible, from history, and your life?
   How do they inspire you to live a better life?

Sarah shares,

"I'm grateful for **sisterhood**.
I'm grateful that God did not create us to live
by ourselves as islands **alone**, but that God
and His infinite wisdom knew that **companionship**
would be a **blessing** to us on our **journey**."

7. When have you tried to go it alone apart from others? What was the result? What role do women play in helping you experience a spiritual breakthrough and growth?

Sarah shares,

"There are **other** women for us to
wrap our arms around—other **teen** moms,
other **divorcees**, other women experiencing
depression and having attempted **suicide**.
Other women who have had **addictions**.
There are more women who need to hear
about this **resurrection power** that
we have experienced."

8. Who is God bringing into your life to be part of the sisterhood of believers? How can you embrace, celebrate, and encourage them through deeper friendship?

9. Reflecting on this *Woman Evolve* study, what's the greatest transformational truth you're walking away with?

CLOSING ACTIVITY

1. Briefly review the video outline and any notes you took.

2. In the space below, write down the most significant thing you gained in this session—from the teaching or discussions.

   What I want to remember from this session is . . .

CLOSING PRAYER TIME

Write a personal prayer that reflects which area of this session's teaching you feel most in need of prayer about.

Father God,

GROUP PRAYER

Leader: *Read this prayer aloud over the group.*

You are so good to us! You love us, You pursue us, You embrace us, and You refuse to let go of us. Forgives us for falling into the comparison trap with other women, for refusing to become vulnerable, for missing out on the deep friendships You designed for us. Make us spiritually alert to all the incredible women You're bringing in to our lives to bless and be blessed by. Thank You for leading us on this Woman Evolve journey—we are grateful. In Jesus' name, Amen.

Leader: *Read these instructions about Personal Study between meetings to the group before dismissal.*

Every session in *Woman Evolve* includes three days of personal study and two days of reading to help you make meaningful connections between your life and what you're learning each week. To make the most of this study, don't forget to work through the material in **the final chapter of the book *Woman Evolve*.**

BETWEEN SESSIONS
PERSONAL STUDY

DAY 1
THE BEST FRIENDS FOR YOU

Long past the age of childbirth, Elizabeth discovers through a series of miraculous events that she is pregnant. Six months later, her relative, Mary, becomes miraculously pregnant, too. The two don't just share a season of pregnancy, they share a bond of sisterhood that will change the world forever.

Read Luke 1:26–28.

1. Why do you think the angel told Mary that Elizabeth was pregnant? What comfort do you think this provided to this unwed teenager?

Read Luke 1:29–35.

2. What is the response to each of the following:

   Mary's response to the news of Elizabeth's pregnancy:

   Elizabeth's response to Mary's greeting:

3. Read Luke 1:36–56. What does Mary declare?

4. What do you think Mary and Elizabeth as soul sisters shared and discussed during their three months together?

5. Who have you bonded with in a spiritual sisterhood because of life events, location, workplace, or church?

6. How has that relationship impacted you and the other person?

7. What do the following verses advise on friendships? Fill in the chart below.

SCRIPTURE	Wisdom for life-giving friendships
ECCLESIASTES 4:9–10	
PROVERBS 12:26	
PROVERBS 17:9	
PROVERBS 22:24–25	
JOHN 15:12–13	
1 THESSALONIANS 5:11	
COLOSSIANS 3:13	

8. Which of these verses is most challenging to you today? Why?

DAY 2
YOU'RE AN OVERCOMER

When it comes to actual women in the Bible, Eve and Mary will always be the greatest of all time for me. But there is another woman I want to introduce you to before our time comes to an end. This woman is not an actual woman but rather a manifestation of a vision that John had while on the island of Patmos.

Most theologians see the vision of this woman as a representation of the church. When I read this story, I can't help but see it as quite literal because the woman represented this beautiful combination of Eve and Mary. The woman in these verses does not have a name. This woman is every woman.

Read Revelation 12:1–6 and Genesis 3:16.

1. How does this woman in Revelation have a hint of Eve in her?

2. How does this woman go from mirroring a hint of Eve's story to Mary's story in verse 5?

3. What does God do to protect, provide for, and sustain the woman?

4. What has God done to protect, provide for, and sustain you during an impossible time?

Read Revelation 12:7–9.

5. Who fights for the woman when she cannot fight for herself?

6. Do you believe God is fighting for you when you cannot fight for yourself? Why or why not?

Revelation 12:13–14.

7. What are the wings God has given you to soar above insecurity, past pain, and deep losses?

Read Revelation 12:15-17.

8. How does God continue to orchestrate the woman's rescue?

9. How is God continuing to orchestrate your rescue?

Sometimes the enemy of our destiny is counting on the fact that we may not know it's possible to have victory over disease, depression, corporations, and oppression. The systems that oppress people are only successful when the people feel they have no other option. Remember that you're a part of a kingdom that has come to destroy the works of every power that dares to keep people marginalized, damaged, broken, or confused—and God has got you every step of the way.

DAY 3
WOMAN EVOLVE!

1. What are three of the most important truths you learned from studying *Woman Evolve*? How have those truths set you free?

2. After reviewing your notes and comments from this guide, what surprises you the most? Why?

3. What's one practical application from *Woman Evolve* that you've already put into practice?

4. What's one practical application from *Woman Evolve* that you would still like to put into practice?

5. How has the Holy Spirit prompted changes in your attitudes, actions, and behaviors because of studying *Woman Evolve*?

6. Who are you excited to share your spiritual journey and growth with who can be inspired too?

SMALL GROUP LEADER'S GUIDE

If you are reading this, you have likely agreed to lead a group through the *Woman Evolve Bible Study*. Thank you! What you have chosen to do is important, and much good fruit can come from studies like this. The rewards of being a leader are different from those of participating, and we hope you find your own walk with Jesus deepened by this experience.

Woman Evolve Bible Study is a six-session study built around video content and small-group interaction and based on the book *Woman Evolve*. As the group leader, imagine yourself as the host of a dinner party. Your job is to take care of your guests by managing all the behind-the-scenes details so that as your guests arrive, they can focus on one another and interaction around the topic.

As the group leader, your role is not to answer all the questions or reteach the content—the video, book, and study guide will do most of that work. Your job is to guide the experience and cultivate your small group into a kind of teaching community. This will make it a place for members to process, question, and reflect—not receive more instruction.

There are several elements in this leader's guide that will help you as you structure your study and reflection time, so follow along and take advantage of each one.

BEFORE YOU BEGIN

MATERIALS

Before your first meeting, make sure the participants have a copy of this study guide so they can follow along and have their answers written out ahead of time. Alternately, you can hand out the study guides at your first meeting and give the group members some time to look over the material and ask any preliminary questions. During your first meeting, be sure to send a sheet around the room and have the members write down their name, phone number, and email address so you can keep in touch with them during the week.

VIDEO STREAMING ACCESS

Additionally, spend a few minutes going over how to access the streaming video using the instructions on the inside front cover of each study guide. Helping everyone understand how accessible this material is will go a long way if anyone (including you) has to miss a meeting or if any member of your group chooses to lead a study after the conclusion of this one!

A few commonly asked questions and answers:

Do I have to subscribe to StudyGateway? NO. When you sign up for Study-Gateway for the first time using **studygateway.com/redeem**, you will not be prompted to subscribe, then or after.

Do I set up another account if I do another study later? NO. The next time you do a HarperChristian Resources study with streaming access, all you need to do is enter the new access code and the videos will be added to your account library.

There is a short video available, walking you through how to access your streaming videos. You can choose to show the video at your first meeting, or simply direct your group to the HarperChristian Resources YouTube channel to watch it at their convenience.

HOW TO ACCESS STREAMING VIDEOS: https://youtu.be/JPhG06ksOn8

GROUP SIZE

Generally, the ideal size for a group is between eight to ten people, which ensures everyone will have enough time to participate in discussions. If you have more people, you might want to break up the main group into smaller subgroups. Encourage those who show up at the first meeting to commit to attending the duration of the study, as this will help the group members get to know one another, create stability for the group, and help you know how to prepare each week.

OPENING ACTIVITY

Each of the sessions begins with a brief opening discussion to prepare hearts and minds for the topic of each of Sarah's talks. Some people may want to tell a long story in response to one of these questions, but the goal is to keep the answers brief. Ideally, you want everyone in the group to get a chance to answer, so try to keep the responses to a minute or less. If you have talkative group members, say up front that everyone needs to limit their answer to one minute.

Give the group members a chance to answer but tell them to feel free to pass if they wish. With the rest of the study, it's generally not a good idea to have everyone answer every question—a free-flowing discussion is more desirable. But with the opening icebreaker questions, you can go around the circle. Encourage shy people to share, but don't force them.

PREPARING YOUR GROUP FOR THE STUDY

Before your first meeting, let the group members know that each session contains three days' worth of Bible study, reflection, and the corresponding chapters to read in the *Woman Evolve* book during the week. While these are each optional exercises, the greatest growth happens when we spend time each day in God's Word. Encourage your group to bring any questions and insights they uncovered while reading to your next meeting, especially if they had a breakthrough moment or if they didn't understand something.

WEEKLY PREPARATION

As the leader, there are a few things you should do to prepare for each meeting:

- *Read through the session.* This will help you to become familiar with the content and know how to structure the discussion times.

- *Decide which questions you definitely want to discuss.* Based on the amount and length of group discussion, you may not be able to get through all of the questions, so choose four to five questions that you definitely want to cover.

- *Be familiar with the questions you want to discuss.* When the group meets, you'll be watching the clock, so you want to make sure you are familiar with the questions you have selected. In this way, you'll ensure you have the material more deeply in your mind than your group members.

- *Pray for your group.* Pray for your group members throughout the week and ask God to lead them as they study His Word.

- *Bring extra supplies to your meeting.* The members should bring their own pens for writing notes, but it's a good idea to have extras available for those who forget. You may also want to bring paper and additional Bibles.

Note that in many cases there will not be one "right" answer to the question. Answers will vary, especially when the group members are being asked to share their personal experiences.

STRUCTURING THE DISCUSSION TIME

You will need to determine with your group how long you want to meet each week so you can plan your time accordingly. Generally, most groups like to meet for either sixty minutes or ninety minutes, so you could use one of the following schedules:

SECTION	60 minutes	90 minutes
INTRODUCTION (members arrive and get settled; leader reads or summarizes introduction)	5 minutes	10 minutes
TALK ABOUT IT (discuss one of the two opening questions for the session)	10 minutes	15 minutes
VIDEO NOTES (watch the teaching material together and take notes)	15–25 minutes	15–25 minutes
GROUP DISCUSSION (discuss the Bible study questions you selected ahead of time)	15–25 minutes	30–40 minutes
CLOSING PRAYER (pray together as a group and dismiss)	5 minutes	10 minutes

As the group leader, it is up to you to keep track of the time and keep things moving along according to your schedule. You might want to set a timer for each segment so both you and the group members know when your time is up. (Note that there are some good phone apps for timers that play a gentle chime or other pleasant sound instead of a disruptive noise.)

Don't be concerned if the group members are quiet or slow to share. People are often quiet when they are pulling together their ideas, and this might be a new experience for them. Just ask a question and let it hang in the air until someone shares. You can then say, "Thank you. What about others? What came to you when you watched that portion of the video?"

GROUP DYNAMICS

Leading a group through the *Woman Evolve Bible Study* will prove to be highly rewarding both to you and your group members. However, this doesn't mean you will not encounter any challenges along the way! Discussions can get off track. Group members may not be sensitive to the needs and ideas of others. Some might worry they will be expected to talk about matters that make them feel awkward. Others may express comments that result in disagreements. To help ease this strain on you and the group, consider the following ground rules:

● When someone raises a question or comment that is off the main topic, suggest you deal with it another time, or, if you feel led to go in that direction, let the group know you will be spending some time discussing it.

● If someone asks a question you don't know how to answer, admit it and move on. At your discretion, feel free to invite group members to comment on questions that call for personal experience.

● If you find one or two people are dominating the discussion time, direct a few questions to others in the group. Outside the main group time, ask the more dominating members to help you draw out the quieter ones. Work to make them a part of the solution instead of the problem.

● When a disagreement occurs, encourage the group members to process the matter in love. Encourage those on opposite sides to restate what they heard the other side say about the matter, and then invite each side to evaluate if that perception is accurate. Lead the group in examining other Scriptures related to the topic and look for common ground.

When any of these issues arise, encourage your group members to follow these words from the Bible: "Love one another" (John 13:34), "If it is possible, as far as it depends on you, live at peace with everyone" (Romans 12:18), and "Be quick to listen, slow to speak and slow to become angry" (James 1:19). This will make your group time more rewarding and beneficial for everyone who attends.

SMALL GROUP LEADER'S GUIDE

SESSION BY SESSION LEADER OVERVIEWS

Session (1) Drop Those Fig Leaves

Scripture covered in this session: Genesis 3:1–8; Jeremiah 1:5; Isaiah 43:25; 1 John 1:9; Ruth 1–4

Chapters to read this week: Introduction, Chapters 1–2

Opening Discussion: Briefly ask group members what they hope to get from this study and what the phrase "Woman Evolve" means to them.

Video Discussion Question choices / notes:

_____

_____

_____

_____

_____

_____

_____

_____

Prayer requests:

```



```

Session ② Damage Control

Scripture covered in this session: Joshua 4:1–9; Genesis 3:16, 20–24; Psalm 42:7

Chapters to read this week: Chapters 2–4

Recap Personal Study Time discussion (if you have time, open with a brief recap of what was learned this past week):

DAY ① — **My Weakness Does Not Define Me** pgs 22–27

> **Question:** Where did you feel God poking you to drop the fig leaf?

DAY ② — **Blotting Out My Transgressions** pgs 28–31

> **Question:** How are you rising up to fight for God's vision for your life?

DAY ③ — **What God Says About Me** pgs 32–37

> **Question:** What did you learn or what was confirmed for you this week about what God really says about you?

Video Discussion Question choices / notes:

_____

_____

_____

Prayer requests:

Session ③ What Are We Doing Today?

Scripture covered in this session: Ephesians 5:8, 6:12; 1 Peter 5:8–9; John 10:10, Matthew 4, 5:14

Chapters to read this week: Chapters 5–6

Recap Personal Study Time discussion (if you have time, open with a brief recap of what was learned this past week):

DAY ❶ — God Wants to Heal Me pgs 48–50

> **Question:** What did you need to know or what do you need to know now?

DAY ❷ — God is Doing Something New in Me pgs 51–54

> **Question:** What is one area where you are coming to see God do a new work and bring about good?

DAY ❸ — I'm Taking that Step of Faith pgs 55–57

> **Question:** How are you following God into the unknown? How are you telling Him where He should take you?

Video Discussion Question choices / notes:

_____

_____

_____

Prayer requests:

Session ④ You Need a Trim

Scripture covered in this session: Genesis 13:1-11; Matthew 16:13–23

Chapters to read this week: Chapters 7–8

Recap Personal Study Time discussion (if you have time, open with a brief recap of what was learned this past week):

DAY ❶ — It's Time to Overcome the Enemy pgs 68-70
   Question: Which piece of armor is most important for you to put on each day?

DAY ❷ — You're a Person, Not a Persona! pgs 71-73
   Question: What was revealed to you about how much God loves you just as you are?

DAY ❸ — Let's Be Fruitful and Multiply pgs 74-77
   Question: What change is the Holy Spirit encouraging you to make to allow His fruit to grow in you?

Video Discussion Question choices / notes:

_____

_____

_____

_____

Prayer requests:

Session ⑤ No Turning Back

Scripture covered in this session: Luke 2:41–50; Philippians 3:12–14; Isaiah 26:3

Chapters to read this week: Chapters 9–10

Recap Personal Study Time discussion (if you have time, open with a brief recap of what was learned this past week):

DAY ❶ — No More Strife In My Life pgs 88–91

> **Question:** When has God shown Himself good in the middle of your strife and what did you learn about His character?

DAY ❷ — I Can't Be All Things to All People pgs 91–93

> **Question:** Where are you most tempted to be the savior rather than allow Jesus to be your Savior?

DAY ❸ — Prayer Is Mighty Powerful pgs 93–97

> **Question:** What about Jesus' prayer life is most impactful to you and how can you emulate Him in your prayer life?

Video Discussion Question choices / notes:

_____

_____

_____

Prayer requests:

Session ⑥ Don't Do It Alone

Scripture covered in this session: Luke 10:38

Chapter to read this week: Chapter 11

Recap Personal Study Time discussion (if you have time, open with a brief recap of what was learned this past week):

DAY ❶ — Make Space for Your Peace pgs 108–111

> **Question:** How does spending time with Jesus stay with you long after you've carried on with your day?

DAY ❷ — You Need Your Goals pgs 112–115

> **Question:** Where are you hearing the clear voice and instruction of God in your life most?

DAY ❸ — You Need to Overcome Setbacks pgs 115–119

> **Question:** How are you coming more into alignment with what God says your focus needs to be?

Video Discussion Question choices / notes:

_____

_____

_____

_____

_____

Final Week of Study: This is your final week of study together. Please plan for time to review prayer requests and get updates on any answered prayers throughout the course of your group meeting together. Go back through each session and ask which session was most impactful to each member of your group. Celebrate triumphs of the Spirit and breakthroughs! Encourage each member to complete the Personal Study Time for this final week and to continue in her revolution as a Woman Evolved!

ABOUT THE AUTHOR

Sarah Jakes Roberts is a businesswoman, bestselling author, and media personality who expertly balances career, ministry, and family. She is the founder of Woman Evolve, a multimedia platform dedicated to engaging and empowering the modern woman of faith. She has been the driving force behind grassroots marketing for films, publications, and community programs that inspire and uplift people of all ages and backgrounds.

Sarah is the daughter of Bishop T. D. Jakes and Mrs. Serita Jakes. Alongside her husband, Touré Roberts, she copastors a dynamic community of artists and professionals in Los Angeles, California, and Denver, Colorado. Together they have six beautiful children and reside in Los Angeles.

COMPANION BOOK TO ENRICH YOUR STUDY EXPERIENCE

Available wherever books are sold

From the Publisher

GREAT STUDIES

ARE EVEN BETTER WHEN THEY'RE SHARED!

Help others find this study:

- Post a review at your favorite online bookseller.

- Post a picture on a social media account and share why you enjoyed it.

- Send a note to a friend who would also love it—or, better yet, go through it with them.

Thanks for helping others grow their faith!

 Harper*Christian* Resources

Chrystal Evans Hurst

Lisa Whittle

Wendy Blight

Sandra Richter

Jada Edwards

Lysa TerKeurst

Karen Ehman

Lynn Cowell

Ruth Chou Simons

Jennie Allen

Christine Caine

Jennie Lusko

Ann Voskamp

Rebekah Lyons

Megan Fate Marshman

Lori Wilhite

Anne Graham Lotz

Lisa Harper

Margaret Feinberg